FRUIT

Wisconsin Poetry Series

Edited by Ronald Wallace and Sean Bishop

FRUIT

BRUCE SNIDER

The University of Wisconsin Press

Publication of this book has been made possible, in part, through support from the Brittingham Trust.

The University of Wisconsin Press
728 State Street, Suite 443
Madison, Wisconsin 53706
uwpress.wisc.edu

Gray's Inn House, 127 Clerkenwell Road
London EC1R 5DB, United Kingdom
eurospanbookstore.com

Printed in the United States of America
This book may be available in a digital edition.

Library of Congress Cataloging-in-Publication Data
Names: Snider, Bruce, author.
Title: Fruit / Bruce Snider.
Other titles: Wisconsin poetry series.
Description: Madison, Wisconsin : The University of Wisconsin Press, [2020] | Series: Wisconsin poetry series
Identifiers: LCCN 2019039056 | ISBN 9780299326746 (paperback)
Subjects: LCGFT: Poetry.
Classification: LCC PS3619.N53 F78 2020 | DDC 811/.6—dc23
LC record available at https://lccn.loc.gov/2019039056

for L
—

Thou art my Father, thou my Author, thou
My being gav'st me; whom should I obey
But thee, whom follow?
—John Milton, *Paradise Lost*

Contents

FRUIT

THE BLUE WHALE HAS THE LARGEST HEART
OF ANY LIVING CREATURE

A human child could stand head high
inside the chambers, crawling through
the valves. The child could burrow
to stare up at the heart's ceiling, the curve
of ventricle, architecture of artery
and vein. Awake to the animal breathing,
the lungs' vast bellow, the thundering ribs
and spine, he could touch his hand
to the walls, the same walls that beat
only six times a minute—slowing further
when the whale surfaces, to five, then four.
A blue whale's heart is a wet muscle
that holds a child, who, when kneeling
in the flesh, might move the way
he'd move through the attic of his boyhood
home, turning to touch the blood-flush
as if touching a hearth where the fire
wavers. He might see a nest of veins
and imagine the tree branches outside
his bedroom window alive with
squirrels and wild birds, or see leaves
tangled in his mother's hair, the star charts
of an ancient people he'd never know.
If a boy stood in a blue whale's heart,
he could make a silence of its beating, a roof
of its speed, a floor of its gentle nature.
He could feel the depths and move
in a darkness few men see, the beast

heaving around him, all shuddering
breath, bone, and muscle, even when
it was dying, beached, twitching
on the sand. And the child could go
on living in the massive heart to wake
each day to flies, the creature's rot,
having made a home of its vanishing.
He could carve his name into the walls
and call it his own, and walk the floors
and kneel before he slept, bending
as men do to ask forgiveness, blessing
the sick, the poor, the hungry, blessing
his mother and father, praying each
night to the one silence, which is God.

I.

HOMO

The Hall of Human Origins, Smithsonian Museum of Natural History

I love you as one grown man can love
another in this room of tooth-nicked
skullcaps, ridged doors to instincts, hunger.
Pinned to walls, the bone sockets flash black:
Erectus, Sapiens. We stand near hand-axe,
cut spine—*Floresiensis, Neanderthal*—grooves
notched into pelvic bowl, spot-lit ribs,
heart's ornament and armor. This, the sign
says, means evolution: spear tips nudging
crumbled bridal wreathes, flint knives
near mating-beads on wire. All morning,
we walk hand in hand, passing leopard
skins, human skins, men huddling
over split logs, learning to make fire.

LITANY FOR MY FATHER'S SPERM

Within an hour most of the five million sperm from a man's ejaculate are dead.

O little hounds
of Delphi. O
dew of youth.
This one carried
ancient fear and sorrow.
It chewed its wormy lips.
This one was
God's absence.
One beat of the hard
old heart. It was
guesswork and the
passage out. It would
have loved peanuts.
It would have
cried itself to sleep.
This one slept
when it should have
awoken. I clawed my way
into the world on its back.
This one nursed
at shadows, shaking
its phantom limbs,
Job alone in the desert,
Moses in his basket freed.

O endless river
of motion,
little Winnebagos
on creation's road,
you're all lightning
and volcano, all
whip-tailed fallout
from The Big Bang.
What do you know
of what it means
to rest? You're
what dies and goes on
dying, blue jays rolling
zeros in the nest.

CHILDLESS

at the coed baby shower

Banners sag at the windows: *welcome baby boy*. You and I listen to a woman
talk about her childless sister. A small plastic infant floats inside each ice
cube. We play guess the baby food. We play pin the sperm on the egg.
Blindfolded, I'm spun around. I stagger sideways, try to pin the lamp.
Everyone laughs. A woman hands you a napkin patterned with storks
wearing sailor hats. They carry blonde-haired infants in their beaks. In Africa,
I want to tell her, storks feed on garbage and are known to eat whole shoes
and metal and strike at children. You pull me onto the porch. Wind shakes
the back pond alive with toad spawn, geese. All morning, the poplars rattle,
repeating green. They hoard their sticky pollen, then release.

FRUIT

I swatted a mob of flies
from the bowl of peaches;
erased, sharpened my pencil, erased
again. Art Class. Indiana. 1986.
Starkey pushed me, scrawled *dick* on
the back of my chair, his broad

shoulders growing broader
by the second. I watched the flies,
how they crawled on
the flushed skin of the peaches.
I drew them, too—were there six
or seven?—dragging my eraser

down my arm as if I could be erased,
as if I might disappear into Starkey's broad
shoulders, his hard mouth. Sex,
I figured, was as tragic as flies
stalled on a bowl's lip near peaches.
I imagined unbuttoning

his shirt, white buttons
I drew, drew again, then erased.
On his chest: hair soft as peach
fuzz or the pale grass edging the road
where he'd punch me, glasses flying
after school; was it 1985 or '86?

Fifteen going on sixteen,
I was a skinny kid with a bad complexion,
reading—for class—*Lord of the Flies*
about a boy named Piggy's erasure.
I longed for the weight of broad
shoulders. Was hunger peaches,

I wondered, or a sketch of peaches?
Was pain just another word for sex?
I walked home down the road
past a dead dog on its way to resurrection,
more proof that a body could be erased
until—*poof!*—nothing but flies.

CREATION MYTH

I'm the great-grandson of a sheep farmer,
child of sumacs, trash trees shedding their ancient scales.
I'm drawn from fair grass on the north end, my molecules
spat from coal and cattle, the Indiana dusk.
I'm notes scrawled on freezer paper,
the one looped oven mitt Aunt Bev crocheted
while the baby lay feverish in its crib. I rise
from a day gone thin as Cousin Ceily,
who wore her cancer wigs to church.
I come from boys unfastening in the 4-H bathroom,
the stink of urinal cakes, dirty hands that scratched an itch.
I breathe in arc welders and air compressors.
I breathe out milk leaking from nurse cows,
Uncle Jake's *spoiled old bitches*. I'm run through
with moths and meth labs, a child of the KKK,
men who lynched Tom Shipp from a split
oak in Marion, August 1930. My cells
carry his shadow swaying over uncut grass.
They carry my second third cousin
cheering in the back. I rise from aphids
in honeysuckle, egg yolks flecked with blood.
Born one humid summer night, my body hums
like a black cricket, transmitting August
across the fields. I sing till my throat bleeds. I smoke
like a pan of scorched sugar. I'll never forget
the miracle of firecrackers, freezer meat, murky
gray lemonade. I'm born to thunder
in the veins, a child of form, a rusted gasket ring, some
disenchanted thing, the promise of a worm.

MY UNCLE'S BARN CAT AS THE SHADOW OF DEATH

She creeps across the hay-strewn floor,
her paws like oarsmen tugging the doomed
fleet toward war. Romans kissed the dying
to taste the last breaths in their mouths.
She hunts, takes what needs be taken.
Daedalus used a serpent's jaw to cut
wood for coffins; she swallows the garter

snake head first. She is everywhere and
nowhere at once, her teeth the first and last
principle, light clouding the sick man's room.
In Carthage guards tossed thieves into
outhouse pits, their blood not yet cold. Here
she crouches, stalks the chicken coop,
cleans her anus with her small pink tongue.

CHILDLESS

The most popular name for newborn girls last year was Sophia. For boys it was Jackson. The astronomer William Herschel discovered a planet and named it Uranus, called it his oldest child. His whole life it drifted 1.6 billion miles away, but at night he could nod to it through his telescope before closing the curtains. When botanists name newly discovered plants, they use binomial nomenclature. Walking near the reservoir, we read the names of trees: *Acer pseudoplantanus, Quercus robur*. Sometimes we make up our own—*Tree-of-weird-hooked-thorns, Tree-of-gouged-black-trunk*. Beside us *Oak-with-pretty-red-leaves* rises as we'll one day rise, the dirt-of-us erupted with seedlings.

ON SWALLOWING THE FOURTH PLAGUE OF EGYPT

I tasted proboscis and mesothoracic wings,
gospel of melon rinds, liturgy
of cheese left uncovered
on the plate. I don't
know how it happened.
I opened my mouth. There:
house fly? crane fly? robber?—
dark speck with compound eyes—
moth fly? fruit or horse?
the dark tremor entered me.
I coughed the smudged
fingerprint of Thomas Hunt
Morgan, his microscope and
rotten bananas, that ebony pebble—
I heard a fly buzz. I choked on all
I'd been trying to say. I don't
know if it was a cluster fly
or a sand fly or a bluebottle. All
I know is that I hacked
until my ears rang with its sermonizing,
this small arrived-at, this dead
head of a coffin nail hammered
into my throat. It brought me
to my knees—O muddied
sequin clutching the hem
of God's dress—no
ordinary angel of my deliverance
to whom I retched and wept and
knelt, as if I'd been blessed.

BECAUSE EDEN, FROM THE HEBREW, MEANT PLEASURE

and lived on in the moment of arousal
when a surge of noradrenalin
flooded the amygdala, the teacher
put a condom on a banana. Inside
each girl, he said, was a wall of shuddering
muscle and an egg that each month
dropped like a red gumball from the vending
machine outside the liquor store. Semen,
he said, was a protein matrix
that could keep alive millions of almost-
babies or a virus that could nest
in your blood. He showed us
pictures of men with sunken faces,
skin gouged with sores. Adam
and Eve, he said, not Adam and Steve.
The boys who laughed loudest
chucked rocks at the church bell beyond
which acres thrummed with the brain
chemistry of the cornfield.
There was lightning, the teacher said,
in our testicles, coyotes in our blood.
At the 4-H fair, Nick kissed me
outside the calving tent, his face at night
the face of all the boys. We could hear
hooves in the stables, look past each other
into the woods. Soon, we knew,
the heifers would be slaughtered,
the tents torn down. For now: sawdust.

For now: stars punched effortless
through sky. In the dark, he drew
a bird on his palm with a ballpoint pen,
moved his hand to make it fly.

CHILDLESS

My friend Mike thinks having kids is vanity, the desire to have one's genetic material—to borrow the evolutionary term—*selected*. When I think of vanity, I think of my father trimming his dark beard. *You get your brains from the Snider side*, he'd say, sitting in his room, oiling his Colts, Winchesters, Enfields. He taught me how to load each one. When I was nine, he gave me my own knife to gut the rabbits. When I was ten, he pushed me into the lake to teach me to swim: *For your son, you'll do the same.* Standing position. Kneeling position. He taught me "rice paddy prone." Smiling, he patted my back. I held up our small slaughter, my teeth stung by chill as I drank from our reflection in the creek bed, more self in my throat than water.

ELLIPSIS, DASH, BULLET POINT

The Remington Arms Company is the oldest continuously operating manu-
facturer in North America and largest US producer of shotguns and rifles.
On March 1, 1873, the company began production of its first typewriter.

I type: SNIDER, feel

                    the barrel's release. Gun-

powder, oil. In the hills,

                    opossum burrow underbrush,

my hands buzzing. I type

                    again, then again and—

my father's face. He scratches

                    his graying beard. Type: YOU

ALWAYS. Type: YOU

                    NEVER take a path,

so uncertain. Where

                    is it headed? Barrel-

thrum. What does silence

                    get you? Leaf-silt, Magnolia cone.

Split red seeds. Type: WHAT

                    DID YOU MEAN? Leaning

back: blood-rush, leaf-rustle.

Cowslip, scab apple. Night-

song of skunk cabbage.

Scuffed and sour. Scuffed

and lean. Type: I'M TRYING

the whole sky swallowed

TO TELL YOU everything

keeps moving. Self

like an echo. Self like

a stone. I reach for

my father, load another

Type: SORRY. Type:

NOT SORRY. Rabbit

slackening the dog's jaws.

CLEANING MY FATHER'S RIFLE

With a soft wire brush, I scrub
darkness from
    the barrel's mouth, erasing
the last
    look of

the doe crouching
           in wet grass, eyes
wide, breathing. I smooth
away clay and oil,

his fingers'
corrosive prints, even meat
    spatter, microscopic
chips of bone. I wipe
    away the field—bees
and pears, crisp-

leaf clover—the slow blue
seam of
    the creek moving
past. I erase the bullet's
velocity,
    the dizzy

stink of flies. Scrubbing
night from
    the weed-choked pond, I erase
the dense

shroud of fog that speaks
his name. I wipe away
his good
            judgment, his better
aim, scouring

loneliness from
    the huckleberry
patch where he knelt to split
the body open,
    lungs glistening in
their bone-cage,
gut steaming

its sour gas. I wipe grasshopper
and mourning
    dove, buzzards circling,
copperheads coiled
in the long grass.
            Nothing can be

left. Not the still heart's center.
Not the blood
    .pooled, clotting. I wipe
away thorn-gash
    and the wild
cherry's deep sweetness, the cold

body as it stiffens, summer
collapsing into
    teeth and hooves, ripeness
and ease—pine
shadow

over his unlaced work
boot, sparrows, smashed
beer can's rusty
        lip. I wipe away
it all, even the entrails
he burns
    in the fire

pit, even their climb toward
the unreachable
    heavens, curling
upward, whitening
to ash.

THEY WILL NOT EAT THE BIRD OF PARADISE

but they will devour the rose, the foxglove,
the lily of the valley, their flat teeth
scouring the crocus to a nub
over cold names and dates. They will not eat
the bird of paradise, but they will
crouch on the cheatgrass and mark the iris
with their urine, and lie on headstones,
chewing their cud. After the grave
diggers have wiped down their shovels,
the furred shapes will rise at dusk from
behind the Wal-Mart, hooves
sinking into mud along Garner's Creek.
Vinegar, garlic, black pepper,
nothing stops their coming from
the long grasses, the old
ones scraping antlers, the young
testing their milk teeth on weeds outside
the embalmer's window as he works late
to disinfect the body, shaving the face
so makeup won't cake the fine hairs.
And the nose arranged just so.
And the anus plugged with cotton,
the mouth filled with paste to make
the lips more pleasing. They will not eat
the bird of paradise, but an old ravaging
will sheer away the tulips and wild lavender.
They will come from the woods around
Elkhart and Albion, the wide
open fields along Route 9, moving
as the dead's new dream of spring.

Such relentless taking. They will not care
about grief, just sweet leaves and the damp
sexual hearts of the flowers, all teeth
and tongues in a dark night
of acorn shells and amaryllis, endless
mouths culling the perfumed
bodies of carnation, clematis, the lilac
bouquets lying heaped and left
nearly rotten by the January rain.

WHY MY FATHER SMELLS LIKE THE NIGHT

Because he lifted the rusted
cutting shears in the name of his
dead brother and the tree limbs
refused to give. Because
he wore Brut, bear scat
and barley, the idle threats
of birds. Because he wore
barn knot and broken, making
anger look easy. His cologne
filled the house with its cheap
drugstore worry. Whiff
of bacon. Whiff of spade-
split turnip. When his brother
died, he cried for days. Because
the world clung to him, spit
sticky and grease fire. Because
he walked out wearing
manly and make-do. Because
his brother once took him fishing
in Ohio. Because when he went
to the graveyard, the pine trees
released their dark scents. Because
what else would grief
smell like if not black
shadows in the cornfield, if not
the moon's slow bone caught
in the bullfrog's throat?

CHILDLESS

at the aquarium

The seahorse bobs alone in the tank. We study its long nose and thorny
crown, the way its tail grasps the soft coral. A sign: *The male's "brood" pouch
can hold over a thousand fertilized young.* All day I imagine bodies inside my
body, each leading to some new us. Later, when we play Scrabble, I spell D-E-
S-I-R-E. You add D for a triple word, feeling moved to the past tense. You
laugh, tell me we're better off than most. It's been ten years in this house, the
spare room still unfinished, the garden a tangle of weeds. Sometimes I wish
we were bowls, stackable, one nesting in the other. After dinner, we drive to
play dolls with our goddaughter, push a truck along a plank of orange blocks
until she laughs. In her books, we read how a squirrel feeds a bear from a
honey pot, how a mother squid drifts in a cloud of ink, babies gathered in her
improbable arms.

AFTER READING THE WIKIPEDIA ENTRY ON HOMOSEXUAL BEHAVIOR IN MOTHS

they're

what the spring
says and keeps

on saying:
        they arrive

departing:

      flirting

near
strobes,

      a thousand

sins eating
through

the priest's robes

INSIDE THE CREATION MUSEUM

A dove hangs from the ceiling.
God: the rod

that holds its head
in place. Plastic hummingbirds,

acrylic fish. Adam beside
Tyrannosaurus Rex.

Blessed are the sheep
that look like sheep.

Blessed, the screws that hold
the trees upright.

Eve stands golden haired,
dusted at night

like the chairs.
Rubber jellyfish, Styrofoam stone.

Moonlight swings
from its black cord. Blessed,

the sow that nurses
nothing, her hammered eyeball

lit with a quiet calling.
Faith's fire,

doubt's smoke-filled haze.
The hawk with its feathers

perfectly sculpted,
dry rags

that fill the lion's chest easily
forgotten—

or set ablaze.

THE AVERAGE HUMAN

breath contains approximately 10^{44} molecules, which, once exhaled,
in time spread evenly through the atmosphere

        so today I took
in the last breaths of James
Baldwin Marie Curie Genghis
Kahn my great-great-grandmother's
breath entering me beside the breath
of a Viking slave boy immolated
on the flames of his master's
burning corpse. I inhaled
African queens Chinese
emperors the homeless
man with the bright blue
coat down the street. If oxygen
is the third most plentiful
element in the universe, moving
through us like Virgil through
the underworld, how long
have I tasted the girl
drowned among cattails near
the murky shore? In ancient Egypt
a priestess packed a corpse with
salt but not before a breath
escaped that two thousand years
later entered me or at least
atoms of it, a molecule. Plato
theorized atoms in 400 BC

and this morning outside
Athens I took in his last breath,
my lungs damp crypts
where Charon's oars dipped
into the black waters of the River
Styx, not knowing who would
pay the ferryman and
with what coin on what tongue.

CHILDLESS

in Rome

In the Vatican, we pause at a goddess of fertility who wears the marble
testicles of bulls. Behind us: children of tourists, a fury of hands. In painting
after painting, another infant cherub, another baby Jesus stares from Mary's
lap. At the hotel, I lay beside you with this body that can never make a
child with your body. We make love, talk about the statues of Hadrian and
Antinous, how our guide described excavated brothels, young men who
sold themselves to Roman soldiers. By morning, we wake refreshed. June
sun glints off old stonework in the villa below, a tobacco tin, oranges in the
trees. Later, in our rental car outside the city, we hold hands, passing acres of
trellised vines, grapes ripening along the highway, arguing for wine.

CHEMISTRY

From the middle Dutch *boele*, which
    means lover, *bully* was a term
of endearment in the sixteenth century,
    which meant that a feudal lord
could take the hand of his love
    under the apple trees in spring
and exclaim: *my bully*, feeling
    adrenaline flood his body as his heart
rate tripled and his palms began
    to release water mixed with urea,
ammonia, salt. Essentially,
    he could feel what I felt over four
centuries later when Ian Starkey
    called me a fag. I was fourteen,
and the next day he kicked me twice,
    spat in my face, took my glasses
and wouldn't give them back.
    And the whole time sweat glands
were developing in our armpits and genitals,
    and our adrenals were releasing
corticosteroids, and something
    about testosterone was why, though
I hated him, I kept imagining
    him with his shirt off. True,
Ian Starkey knew how to hurt me,
    but I doubt he knew why he was doing it

or that we feel pain when neurons
in the brain convert an electrical
signal to a chemical signal and back
again, which is also what allows
us to feel a kiss or my brain
to take strange comfort imagining
all the boys of the world leaning into
the strong arms of their tormentors
in spring under the apple blossoms, saying
I forgive you, saying: *I can never forgive you,*
saying, *my enemy, my bully, my love.*

ON BILLY LUCAS, WHO HANGED HIMSELF
IN HIS GRANDMOTHER'S BARN

The horse stall still holds his shadow
as the hayloft holds last fall's bound hay.
All day the field offers its usual mercies:
rust on a sardine tin, quick worm
in the crack willow bud. Wind shakes
the picked-over fruit. Here lies
a dog's bone, notched by teeth.
Here: speckled eggs, shit and straw.
Somewhere a body is hammered
into something new, beyond chain saws,
grain elevators, and the Pizza Hut off Route 9.
Alders weep leaves into churchyards,
Jesus and the squares of lime Jell-O.
Farm boys roll joints in the back acre, using
pages from the King James, lighting Luke,
Matthew, His words rolling upward. Soon
night will take it all, even the baler broken
down by the roadside, even the jack pine's
high needles that no one can touch. Gone,
the field says, means gone, what's here
about to go. Goodbye to the day
as it releases the dew's dew-ness
dissolving with an enviable freedom,
blind to the cold snap, and already snow.

DEVOTIONS

1.

Nothing passes, Lord, but what you allow.
Mornings the milky sap on my knuckles
burns. Last night the piglets fought then suckled
in the barn. Still no word. Our one cow
grazes but won't come in. The pamphlets say:
Patience is required. I say, let's try again
but John blames the state, the neighbors, the way
we wrote our bios, filling out the forms.
Across the road our neighbor starts his truck
while God, feather by feather, downs a wren—
swollen, its black eyes shiny, small dark tongue.
In the drainpipe, something slithers wet and stuck.
A racerunner? A ground skink shedding skin?
Lizards, John tells me, *can't bear live young.*

2.

John tells me: *Lizards can't bear live young.*
Another of God's mysteries: hard rain
muddying the corn. The kind woman
at the agency said, *It takes longer for same-
sex couples.* Trash smoke rises like prayer,
the neighbor burning insulation from his shed.
He shows his son how to bind fence where
a crippled chicken pecks at scattered feed.
They talk, lean close. Rusted toys fill
the side yard: old trucks, a bicycle tire,
a punctured red bucket now a sieve.
In the back acre, ram mounts ewe, the whole
field coupling late spring. When John walks by,
I kiss him. Most days we keep to ourselves.

3.

I kiss him most days. We keep to ourselves
by the roadside. Two greasy boxes; a sign:
FREE. We take the runt, her warm body beside
us in the truck, milk-breathed and unwormed.
I imagine her shuddering out of the womb, wet
ground covered with slime. Strange to think
of her moving inside some animal's gut,
the source of each day's warm alien kick.
At home John makes her a bed from old
field shirts, a soap and vinegar bath for fleas
while in my lap she chews my hand and shivers.
I brush her fuzzy scruff, the too-large head.
She nips at my finger that holds a piece of cheese,
her wet tongue asking what a man can mother.

4.

Even I doubt how a man can mother
when I see the neighbor shout, chuck a stone
at his son. When I shoot him a look, he turns:
Mind your own business. The hot sun withers
the peonies John planted on the side of the hill,
dirt gone hard with the sudden change of weather.
Sweating I mow the lawn, pick up shell
casings in the yard, the crow's strict feathers.
All day, I want to break something, stick
a fork in the fan blades to feel the pinch.
Coming home late again from the shop,
John carries two rabbits slung from a hook.
He cleans, for hours, his rifle on the porch.
Above us: the moon rises. An easy shot.

5.

Above us the sun rises, bright and hot,
steaming the back pond where black flies stall.
In the pasture, our neighbor castrates his bulls
using a spreading tool with red rubber slats.
The restless cattle graze an unshorn meadow.
On TV: a baby in Toledo in a locked car.
The mother went to work and forgot, windows
up in summer's heat. The camera blurs
over the lot as a medic lifts the blanketed heap
from the back seat in the crew's full view.
Gawkers circle. The mother weeps. Watching,
I can peaches, letting the pale fruit darken.
Beyond the window, bulls still graze the field.
They feed. The bloodless sacks swing, blacken.

6.

Steer feed. The bloodless sacks hang, blackened.
On the radio: Haggard's "I'd Rather Be Gone."
John tends to ordinary things: replaces the drain
pipe in the kitchen sink, sharpens knives again.
I watch the neighbor teach his son to paint
the tool shed all afternoon. Soon, they wrestle,
throw a ball, the boy laughing into his father's chest.
In the paper I read the births and deaths,
hear a sudden hammering from behind,
John cursing the warped floorboards, pushing hard
the back door, which still won't budge an inch.
Again, today no miracles at hand,
just, in the field, wrens who stab at milkweed pods,
a nuthatch bargaining from its split branch.

7.

A nuthatch bargains from its split branch.
Our neighbor stops by, complains our fence
breaks his field. It must be moved eight inches.
The puppy—*Annie* we call her—pushes
her nose in everything, the front yard, the garden,
finds, across the road, the neighbor's trash,
drags stripped wire, egg shells that harden
like the bones she buries off his porch.
I want to say we are consoled by her,
but each day John jumps when he hears the phone.
We walk over and over down the worn
path to the empty mailbox: *Maybe soon.*
Some nights we make love. We sleep arm to arm.
We wake to our neighbor yelling at his son.

8.

Again, we wake, our neighbor yelling at his son,
poor kid standing by the porch. Tracking mud,
he backs from the shouting, his father's raised fist.
Later, I will see him sulking near our feed shed,
knotting an old piece of garden hose, kicking dust.
I'll smile, ask if he's OK. But right now,
I listen to John's quiet breathing beside me.
Faith, they say, is Abraham asked to slaughter
his boy on a mountaintop. But sometimes
it's just the peeling shed in gray weather,
the leather harness softened, then gone rough.
All day today, the back pond will teem with carp.
The clover will brighten. For now, we lie together
into late morning. Some days, it is enough.

TWIN PEAKS BAR, SAN FRANCISCO

the country's first gay bar with windows

Ralph's working late again, people walking past
the window where I sit and stir my drink,
his face another shape against the glass.

Thirty years ago he still lived in La Place
and each spring helped his father plant the wheat.
Now I watch him at the bar, people walking past

as he makes cosmos, sidecars, even a furnace blast—
its secret (so he claims) is one-part gasoline—
his face another shape against the glass.

He's seen it all, the Castro's fall, the clash
of riots, Harvey Milk, parades that lit the street,
though he kept working, people walking past

porn shops, bakeries, the plague that slashed
his boyfriend, Ted, the Greek masseur,
his face another shape beyond the glass.

He calls (sometimes) his brother in La Place,
remembers barley packed in crates they'd ship
to New York, Cincinnati, Montreal. *What's past*

is past, is all he says, adding a splash
of dry vermouth, an olive speared right through
its brined and pitted heart inside the glass.

He has a walk-in flat, at fifty-five, a high firm ass
he chalks up to the gym and carrot juice
(twice a day). *So many people can't get past*

the loss, he shrugs and takes my cash.
You'll learn that, Doll. He wipes the bar,
my own face taking shape against the glass

that holds his quickened hands still mixing
grenadine, lemon juice, rum into a silver flask.
He turns toward all the people walking past
and shakes and stirs, and fades into the glass.

CHILDLESS

Our three-year-old goddaughter takes off her underwear, runs through the house. She's a bottle rocket over the church fence, coffee grounds on the sofa cushions, the one cupboard door unlatched. She rages like the Wabash River, leaves her muddy footprints on the stairs. She's the tree house we made with splintered boards, part freckled smoke bomb, part struck match, the sputtering candle that melts and melts. She's the dandelion spitting its fury of seed: *me, me, me.* Who else?

TOY BOX

A boy can love his sister's doll,
touch its swiveling
legs, knots of acrylic hair, and imagine
this is the child he's given
birth to in his closet
while his parents are asleep. He can nurse
and soothe it; and it will say: *mother,*
teaching him its dead eyes
and its plastic body
as he puts on
its stillness without fear or grief.
When a boy loves his sister's doll,
he can pretend he's not cutting the grass
or cleaning the garage
with his father.
He can step into the doll as a boy
might enter a small town,
and smell the dark
rain-streaked streets, know the bare
shop windows, the courthouse
clock chiming
in the doll's cold hard face. All day
he can imagine its mask
of unknowing. When he buries it
behind the garage
so his sister can't give it
to the neighbor girl, he can dream
the ground, its stones
and lost marbles, the small
pink mouth
crying: *mother, mother.*

SHELTER

1.

Easy buddy, Mom says to the pit bull mix
with the broken back as she slips
an arm behind its neck, strokes a dewclaw
as she talks, cradles the muzzled jaw.
This is what she likes the least, waiting
for the syringe to fill, looking down
at it trussed and shaking. She runs
a hand down the warm side, hesitating
as she checks her supplies: sheet, clamp,
metal bucket (for when the bladder goes).
She turns up the plastic radio,
leans across the table, cramping
fur and bone as, again, the day winnows
to a whimper, a push: *There you go.*

2.

I tug at her arm, then push—she let's go
of my hand in the changing room,
bends to try a pink dress, stiff lacey hem.
I read comics, step into the hall, rows
of other rooms: the mannequins' hard flesh,
waxen hands opening. *Don't touch,*
she says, when I tug at the hanging dresses,
ghostly bodies floating. Flat-chested,
I lean on the racks, press against sleeves,
skirts, a sequined bodice. Is it my head
or the mannequin's bald plastic
snagged in the mirror? Unreal, we
rise together, mix of thighs, hips, breasts,
my own face grown stranger in the glass.

3.

Each one made stranger by the glass
tube, a needle in its gums, the Lab
abandoned, left for dead, burns and scabs
that won't matter once the time is past.
Afterwards, she holds each head, lets
it cool—*just to be sure*—watches fleas
and nits run off the legs, closes the eyes,
settles the neck, moves on to the next.
Sometimes the newborns jerk or spasm,
muscles tightening, a kind of cough.
Is it the soul she imagines? Something sour
breaking loose as she leans to comfort them?
Unfastening muzzles and leather cuffs,
she checks her watch, marking the hour.

4.

On her desk the clock ticks, marking the hour
my father comes home. She dabs
Wild Rose behind each ear, green scarab
fastened at her neck, cream to soften pores.
Noon air swims with the sudden fuss
of perfume, blush, the nylon's snag.
When she's not looking, I touch the canvas bag
that holds my father's stash: Jameson
in the drawer under the armoire's mirror.
I turn when she turns, powder streaking silk,
light peeking through cracks as it falls
like his belt, hooked silent now over
its nail. The lipstick tube uncoils. I hold it
to my mouth. *Shhh*, she says, *I won't tell.*

5.

There's only so much she can tell,
an old Lab with a lame leg. It doesn't move,
steadying its milky eye. What will prove
its end? A car, the heat? Her own hand
at the vein? Mange, heart disease, pink eye—
she knows the score—tumors, chiggers, the gas—
standing at the table, naming what's passed.
She keeps records on the pad beside
her grocery list: bread, chips, cottage cheese,
erasing as she stoops to write, *worms, stroke,*
cancer, then *X,* then *X* again. She heaves
another stack of files on her desk, leans
to roll a fresh cigarette, the trail of smoke
mixing with their scent on her sleeve.

6.

Unfixing the doll's tent, velvet sleeve
that holds Melinda, Melissa, Mary.
She brushes their hair. I neaten each wiry
ribbon, cut a skirt from my father's old glove.
A drop of glue mends the split in Mary's face
but not the welt he left on my arm.
Between the hands, I pile chipped legs,
red lips, a heap of wide glass eyes. Some parts
just can't be saved. *It's OK,* she says, leaning
to get the tray with its cubed sugar, darts
of lemon. I hold Mary's head over
her cracked torso, the teakettle whistling
like my gym teacher in his blue shorts:
boys on one side, girls on the other.

7.

Suits on one side, dresses on the other,
the dark closet opens. She lays out
her clothes, ready for her shift tonight.
She folds his shirts, irons creases in his pants.
In the living room, she scrubs the mess:
stains on the armchair, a heap of crushed
cigarettes, throws his empties in the trash.
I help her sort through what's left
of the lamp he smashed, his spare flask
spilled where he's passed out again. Splayed
on the sofa, he snores till late afternoon,
still in last night's clothes. She vacuums
around him. When his boss calls, she says:
He's sleeping. She says: *He's not well today.*

8.

They could be sleeping, so still today.
Stacked in twos, they burn in the back.
At first the rising stink made her sick,
but now she covers her mouth, throws
them whole into the incinerator,
adding what the city's brought, feral cats,
a dead raccoon, roadkill, a nest of rats.
They burn the same, some straighter
than the rest, but all a heap of ash
in the end, and smaller than you'd think.
Just one more, she tells herself, scraping the tray
as she sweeps the oven out, washing
the overhead lights that flash and wink
at all she says, and all she does not say.

ELEGY FOR THE GIRL I WAS

For the first six weeks following conception, all human embryos develop as female.

Little girl of my unbecoming, your ghost moves

through me. You, a kink in my walk, tiptoe through

the halls of me, vanishing down the lane. Girl of

my thousand selves, let the black waters wash over

you, who knew neither boy nor man, who

knows the graveyard I have always been, sealed

crypt of me, your ending, where it all began. Little

Ghost, remember me—mother: *almost, almost.* O paper

onto which I'm written, script I won't learn. Fate

folds, unfolds your cold limbs. Into my warm

marrow, you reach—cell of my cells—and burn.

CHILDLESS

My friend now calls the fetus inside her *the parasite*. She retches over the toilet all night, suffers weeklong migraines. Hospitalized, she tells me she's read about a kind of spider who gives birth, then surrenders her body, allowing the hatchlings to swarm her and feed. When we see our goddaughter, I notice her small craggy incisors, shards of calcified tissue evolved to tear and slice. She eats avocados and fruit chews, whole sleeves of saltines. When we take her to the zoo, she eats cold gelatinous hot dogs, licks an ice cream cone in front of the pen where a single stork drinks from a chipped dish. It's missing its left eye, has a broken foot. The plaque says, *Origin: Middle East*, rescued from poachers who shoot the massive birds for sport. It walks the pen, a flash of skeletal wings, limping like some creature we've imagined, some myth of itself struggling back to life.

LITANY FOR MY FATHER'S GUNS

This one I confess my doubts to.

This one calls my name.

This one is immaculate and without apology.

It dreams of intestines in grass.

What can be said of this one, with its scored barrel, its safety catch?

This one moved through mangrove swamps, the Mekong River Delta.

It floated down the Red River.

It shot the Vietnamese.

This one he used as a tent stake, this one a crutch.

This one he taught the secrets of beauty.

This one says: *dirt-dirt-dirt.*

This one dreams the cold rooms of winter.

It remembers bear tracks, the dog's piss steaming snow.

This one tastes backwash and bitter saliva.

It has a rotgut strap, a gaping metal eye.

It remembers how he ate the testicles and ground the snout to cheese.

It says: *use me.*

It says: *please.*

STILL LIFE WITH COWS

I've learned my own nature
watching them stand in alfalfa,

docile, wide eyed, tongues lolling.
I've put my hands on their

udders and known their milk
warm on my fingers, heard

my uncle call them: *Peanut,
Izzie, Clementine.* I've known

their moods and their silences,
and, in autumn, smelled their shit

mix with the cool-season grasses
and felt happy simply when they

licked my hand. I've known
what I'd call devotion, picking

ticks off their hindquarters,
rubbing their flanks with salve. Yes,

I have held them as their blood
clotted the drain thick as honey.

And I've cut belly to brisket
to tail. I've watched my uncle

fire the black kettles, then boil
their kidneys to a richer broth.

I have knelt slowly beside them
in a field as one might to propose

and held a rifle to their heads, hearing
their grunts and sighs, my sweet

sluggish brides coming to me
shyly, and in their veils of flies.

IT'S THE DOG

In the documentary about the man talking
about his dead lover, it's the dog
I feel saddest for, the way he roams
the house, chewing the dead lover's slippers,
scratching the back door. I don't know
if it's grief the dog feels so much
as a kind of confusion,
which I guess is grief, or an aspect of it.
My neighbor Beth thinks dogs grieve
the same way people do, but she also
thinks the saddest thing in the documentary
is the dead man's sister
who can't stop cleaning things
with ammonia-soaked rags: doorknobs,
faucets, the porcelain tub.
You could say Beth's more of a dog person,
but she cried for days
when she found her cat Lucy bloated
and stinking in the tomato bed.
She still dreams about Lucy—fat, lazy,
slinking along the sliding glass door.
Sometimes Lucy meows or whispers her name.
Sometimes she floats into the trees,
a hairy balloon. Beth isn't sure
what this means, but wishes she knew.
I wish the man in the documentary
could stop carving the leg of lamb,
crying. He doesn't know
how to carve lamb. If his dog
were mine, I'd rub his silky neck

and give him a bone. When Beth
comes by with her dogs,
sometimes she brings bones.
Sometimes she's sad. Sometimes I am.
Sometimes we play Chase the Ace
or Scrabble. We make dinner
and talk about her dead cat or the movie
we just saw. Sometimes we can't hear a thing
with all the barking.

CHILDLESS

Just the two of us, some days I love you without interruption. Each evening I say your name. Forgive me this rough June sky. Forgive me this constant quarrel. I want huckleberries and endless speed. I want to watch your night sky, your harsh sparks flaring. The whole world teems with banks and libraries, so many swallows in the courthouse bells. The moon rises. A false egg waits in the weasel's nest. Everywhere there are stories of pain and worry. There is you, and butter on my toast.

AT THE SPERM BANK

For fifty bucks you sat there never thinking
what you'd sold—your mother's green eyes,
your father's head for math, his heavy
drinking. Some part of you hadn't lived yet
might not die, abandoned on a day with so much
you'd forget—the time, the shirt you wore—
though you recall blushing as you handed
the nurse your cup with its small embarrassment
of riches. And you can see her face. And you
remember driving home, how your body hummed
the urge of damp soil: ferment, thorn
and hay, how all of April moved through you,
ragweed tossing pollen in a pale froth, leaning
at the fence break, just giving it away.

PRAYER FOR THE BEAR MY FATHER SHOT

It hunted squirrel,
climbed the vast walnut,

knew the silence
of the badger in the wood.

It tasted sour raspberries,
also their thorns.

Mornings it drank
from streams and nuzzled its young.

Forgive its trespasses.
When it came to the campsite,

tore open our cooler
and cracked the lantern top,

it knew not what it did.
Forgive how it bent the tent stakes,

how it howled, spit, crawled
on all fours. And, God,

forgive my father,
because his heart is old

but unfailing, and his vengeance
is just like yours.

ELEGY FOR THE BULLY

You have always been nosebleed
    and nail-bite, the spit-shined halls
where you harvested us with your tribal
    clang. Too long we saw your face
in every shadow, felt the whole forest
    await your arrival like a nagging frost.
We hid from you in toilet stalls,
    quit band to avoid the music
room where you waited near your
    locker. Back then, there was nothing
we could say. In death we greet you
    now as brothers, your dark
silence wailing from those glittering
    trumpets we never learned to play.

HEAVEN AND EARTH

I've been reading how scientists mapped
the human genome using computers

to sketch the five-carbon sugars

deep in my double

helix the way early
mapmakers once sketched trade

routes along the Indian Ocean with ink

made of animal glue and bone-
black pigment.

I guess maps even stop us

from getting lost in our own bodies, wanting
as we do to name everything, Adam

pointing *giraffe, zebra, mongoose.*

Now we're naming the animals
in ourselves—97 percent

of our DNA shared with chimpanzees,

21 percent roundworms.
Turns out a map

of the zoo is a map of our bodies—locked

cages, hours marked for feeding. Or maybe

it's a map of the graveyard
for pets on Hawthorne Street:

the neighbor's dead cat

hissing our cells. We know
in ancient Egypt cats were spirit guides

along with frogs and hawks,
but the earliest maps

of heaven held no place for animals. *All
come from dust,*

and to dust all return. Of course

Saint Francis preached to them

and Ptolemy

put them in the stars—*taurus, lupus, scorpius*—
so geneticists could one day

put them in us, who are also made

of stars. *The end of all flesh
come before me,*

I can almost hear God say

as I sink into a hot bath,
riding the flood while

inside me two

by two
wild horses stamp, wolves

howl, and somewhere a dove

rises, wings
quickening, an olive

branch heavy in its beak.

MENDEL ON HIS DEATHBED

1884

His sickbed reeks of camphor, and the bells
throb across Saint Thomas and the hills.
He rubs his temple.
All afternoon: fever, chills.
A young monk looks after his sour mood,
delivers a fried egg sandwich, boiled cod.
It should not only be your jaws that chew food,
but your ears that thirst for God.
He pushes back the tray,
rubs his woolen slippers on the parquet floors.
What, at this late hour, can he leave
behind? What children
other than his birds and plants, those peas—
labeled by seed and variety—
always the peas rising like spirits of the dead?
He's done with them—
the mice he bred
the bishop thought too vulgar
for a priest, too bodily, animals kept in cages
in his two-room flat, the stench of cedar
chips flaunting
how he watched the mesh
of them twined together, the mounting
rages of fur and flesh.
Soon the brothers will dine at the long refectory
table where even from down the hall
he'll hear the clatter of cutlery and glass.
What words will fall
from their lips when his soul finally passes

tangled as the grapevines
in the icy gardens below?
He thinks of the men and women
embracing in the village beyond the snow,
and the rabbits in heat in their cages,
the profligate vegetables
given to God's mysteries.
Soon, if judged worthy, he'll know
the answers. Why temptations, women?
Why so many children of the poor?
Nodding off, he thinks of the Cistercian nuns
who lived here once, how
their bodies, cloaked
and shapeless, threw
such shadows on the floor.

CHILDLESS

Storks have no voice box and are technically mute, I say, trying to distract my friend Dave, who's just returned from visiting his father in the Alzheimer's unit: *He doesn't even know me.* Storks, I tell him, are the largest flying birds of the Americas and are believed to have risen fifty million years ago, almost forty million years before man. I tell him an adult Marabou has an average wingspan of nine feet, that most eat crickets, small shrews, that sometimes rubber bands mistaken for earthworms can cause a fatal blockage. *You spend too much time on the internet.* I tell him the Greeks made killing a stork punishable by death, but the Romans believed storks never died. Instead, storks flew to an island where they became people. I describe their vast migration, the stab of beaks in a limitless sky, infinite selves of white feathers. *It's genetic. I guess it's a blessing I don't have kids.* For the ancient Chinese, I say, the stork was a sacred bird. In graveyards outside Shenyang, it's etched onto hundreds of tombstones: wings tucked, head bowed, emblem of a grateful man.

CREATION MYTH

When I think of your millions of sperm
extinguished inside me, I remember
reading that the ancient Pythagoreans
believed semen was liquefied brain, a drop
of pure human thought making
its way out of one body into another.
And for a moment I feel myself
filled with your thinking—fragments
of Green Lantern comic books and
old Spanish quizzes, our first awkward kiss.
I teem with your fears and hopes
released from their spigot of yearning
until *I* am what you are thinking,
and I unfold like your final thought,
your last hypothesis with legs and a face
and arms that even now reach over
and over, in the darkness, to be proved.

TERRITORY

All day I've followed roads. Have I come that far?
Terre Haute, Greencastle. Kokomo's not close, but not far.

My father once took me to Muncie.
We drove all the back roads, but not far.

He showed me the old sow in the cattle chute,
the hot electric prod. Burning fur rose, but not far.

Why was Route 9 so full of holes? Why towns with names
like Solitude, Economy? He headed toward Paradise, but it was far.

Sometimes he pointed out Holsteins and Guernseys.
Wandering the fenced fields, they couldn't get far.

Once, he found a cow's placenta in the grass,
a shiny red flag. The new calf consoled: *not far, not far.*

Each Sabbath he drove back from church.
Heaven rang in his ears: so close, yet so far.

At night, in his room, he read The Book:
And on the last day, I will raise him up—and far.

After rain: worms rose like black veins. In the yard,
he worked his Ford. The church bells rang from afar.

For years, he sold *auto* and *life*. His territory:
Auburn to *Fort Wayne*. He always drove fast, but not far.

He gave me, at birth, his name—*Bruce*—so I could follow him.
But where do you follow the dead? And how far?

ONE DAY, HE SAID, I'D CARRY ON THE FAMILY NAME

I know my father's stooped back
is my back, my lungs filling
with his breath like ground
cisterns collecting water deep
below the frost line. Each night
I pull off shoes, unlace
the creak of him from my ankles.
What in me, I wonder, is *me*
as the world goes on copying itself—
black seeds sprouting green,
egg sacks on the gray spider.
I walk to where iron gates open
to the corner graveyard and
the stones say: Snider, Snider, Snider.

FRUTTI DI MARE

Alone, finally, me and you
together, first time in a long week.
We stand in the kitchen cutting
chunks of halibut, fresh crab meat.
Pressing hard, I cleave a stubborn
clam, slice my finger. *More,*

my blood seems to say, *more*
across onions, the counter, while you
grab paper towels, stubbornly
stanch the flow, my knees gone weak.
Hours later, red permeates
the makeshift bandage, the cut

gaping as an ER doctor cuts
sterile thread to sew it up. *No more
knives for you,* he says. I meet
his spectacled eyes, then yours.
We laugh. How many weeks?
you ask. Pain? Infection? your stubborn

worried voice less stubborn
in this light. Home again, you clean cutlery,
say the grass needs mowing this week,
then stand sorting bills and more
while I, looking up at you,
think about that day, years ago, we met,

remembering our young selves, their unmet
needs—raw, impulsive, newborn—
hungry for our bodies, for a me and you.
Now, on the sofa, unsexy, my cut
hand elevated on a pillow, I ask for more
ice and can see the weeks

ahead of laundry, quarrel, devotion, weeks
of living where we meet
what we are and more,
this day and daily-ness reborn
in me and the map of stitches on my cut
finger that points to you.

Acknowledgments

Thanks to the following journals where some of the poems first appeared, often in earlier forms:

The Adroit Journal: "Because Eden, from the Hebrew, Meant Pleasure"

American Poetry Review: "It's the Dog"

Arkansas International: "One Day, He Said, I'd Carry on the Family Name"

The Book of Scented Things: 100 Contemporary Poems about Perfume (Jehanne Dubrow and Lindsay Lusby, eds): "Why My Father Smells Like the Night"

Cherry Tree: "Toy Box," "At the Sperm Bank"

Cincinnati Review: "Creation Myth [I'm the great-grandson of a sheep farmer …]"

Columbia Poetry Review: "Ellipsis, Dash, Bullet Point," "Prayer for the Bear My Father Shot," "Cleaning My Father's Rifle"

Copper Nickel: "Childless [Banners sag at the windows …]," "Childless [Storks have no voice box …]," "Childless [Our three-year-old goddaughter …]"

Harvard Review: "Elegy for the Girl I Was," "Litany for My Father's Sperm"

The Kenyon Review: "Chemistry," "Fruit," "On Billy Lucas, Who Hanged Himself in His Grandmother's Barn"

The Journal: "Inside the Creation Museum," "The Blue Whale Has the Largest Heart of Any Living Creature"

New England Review: "They Will Not Eat the Bird of Paradise"

Pleiades: "Litany for My Father's Guns"

PN Review: "Twin Peaks Bar, San Francisco"

Poetry: "Devotions"

Provincetown Arts: "Homo"

San Francisco Chronicle: "After Reading the Wikipedia Entry on Homosexual Behavior in Moths"

South Florida Poetry Review: "Childless [In the Vatican, we pause ...],"
    "Childless [Just the two of us ...]," "Creation Myth [When I think of
    your millions ...]"

Southeast Review: "Shelter"

Still Life with Poem: Contemporary Natures Mortes in Verse (Jehanne Dubrow
    and Lindsay Lusby, eds): "Still Life with Cows"

Threepenny Review: "The Average Human," "Mendel on His Death Bed"

Virginia Quarterly Review: "Territory," "Elegy for the Bully"

Willow Springs: "Heaven and Earth," "On Swallowing the Fourth Plague of
    Egypt"

ZYZZYVA: "Childless [The seahorse bobs alone ...]," "Childless [My friend
    now calls the fetus ...]"

For support during the writing of this book, thanks to the University of
San Francisco, my colleagues in the English Department and the MFA
Program in Writing, and the USF Faculty Development Fund. Thanks to
Eavan Boland and Stanford University's Wallace Stegner Program, the James
Merrill House Committee, the Amy Clampitt House and the Berkshire
Taconic Foundation, the Corporation of Yaddo, the Virginia Center for the
Creative Arts, George Washington University and the Jenny McKean Moore
Writer-in-Washington fellowship, the Faculty Resource Network at New
York University, and the American Academy of Rome for their generosity to
Fellow Travelers.

Special thanks to Robin Marantz Henig and her book *The Monk in the
Garden*, which was crucial to my understanding of Gregor Mendel's life and
informed my writing of "Mendel on His Deathbed."

Thanks also to friends who provided indispensable support, editorial
and otherwise: Ayad Akhtar, Lynn and Jeff Callahan, Nan Cohen, Reid
and Helen Dorwin, Jehanne Dubrow, Keith Ekiss, Robin Ekiss, Christian
Guillette, Maria Hummell, Sara Michas-Martin, Lisa Moore, Doug Powell,
David Roderick, Kristina Schubert, Jane Shore, Glori Simmons, Susan
Steinberg, and Ryan Van Meter.

Thanks to Beth Chapoton, who inspired "It's the Dog" and to whom the poem is dedicated.

Thanks to Ron Wallace, Sean Bishop, and the University of Wisconsin Press for their continuing faith in my work.

Thanks to my parents and the rest of my family for their unflagging love and support.

Thanks to Lysley for Italy, gin, and driving.

And, finally, thanks to Shara Lessley, my Marco Polo coworker, first and foremost reader, forever friend.

Wisconsin Poetry Series
Edited by Ronald Wallace and Sean Bishop

(B) = Winner of the Brittingham Prize in Poetry
(FP) = Winner of the Felix Pollak Prize in Poetry
(4L) = Winner of the Four Lakes Prize in Poetry

The Golden Coin (4L) • Alan Feldman

Immortality (4L) • Alan Feldman

A Sail to Great Island (FP) • Alan Feldman

The Word We Used for It (B) • Max Garland

A Field Guide to the Heavens (B) • Frank X. Gaspar

The Royal Baker's Daughter (FP) • Barbara Goldberg

Gloss • Rebecca Hazelton

Funny (FP) • Jennifer Michael Hecht

Queen in Blue • Ambalila Hemsell

The Legend of Light (FP) • Bob Hicok

Sweet Ruin (B) • Tony Hoagland

Partially Excited States (FP) • Charles Hood

Ripe (FP) • Roy Jacobstein

Saving the Young Men of Vienna (B) • David Kirby

Ganbatte (FP) • Sarah Kortemeier

Falling Brick Kills Local Man (FP) • Mark Kraushaar

Last Seen (FP) • Jacqueline Jones LaMon

The Lightning That Strikes the Neighbors' House (FP) • Nick Lantz

You, Beast (B) • Nick Lantz

The Explosive Expert's Wife • Shara Lessley

The Unbeliever (B) • Lisa Lewis

Slow Joy (B) • Stephanie Marlis

Acts of Contortion (B) • Anna George Meek

Bardo (B) • Suzanne Paola

Meditations on Rising and Falling (B) • Philip Pardi

Old and New Testaments (B) • Lynn Powell

Season of the Second Thought (FP) • Lynn Powell

A Path between Houses (B) • Greg Rappleye

The Book of Hulga (FP) • Rita Mae Reese

Why Can't It Be Tenderness (FP) • Michelle Brittan Rosado

Don't Explain (FP) • Betsy Sholl

House of Sparrows: New and Selected Poems (4L) • Betsy Sholl

Late Psalm • Betsy Sholl